TO:

....

FROM:

....

DATE:

....

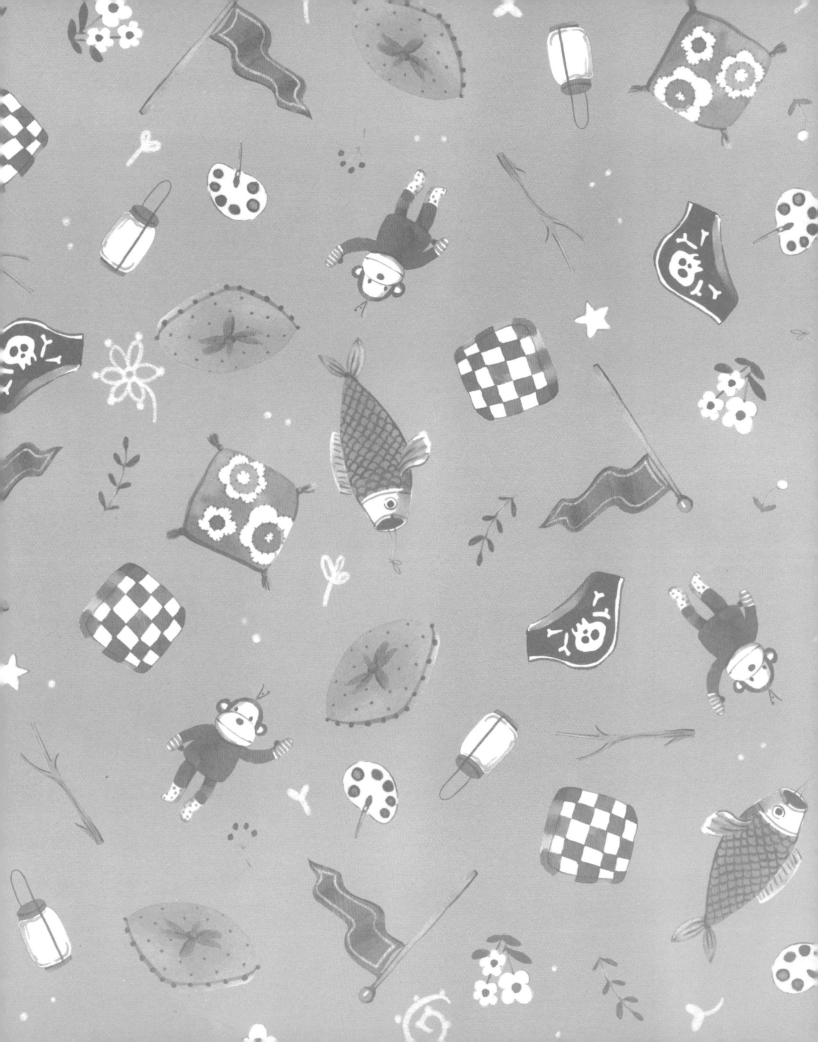

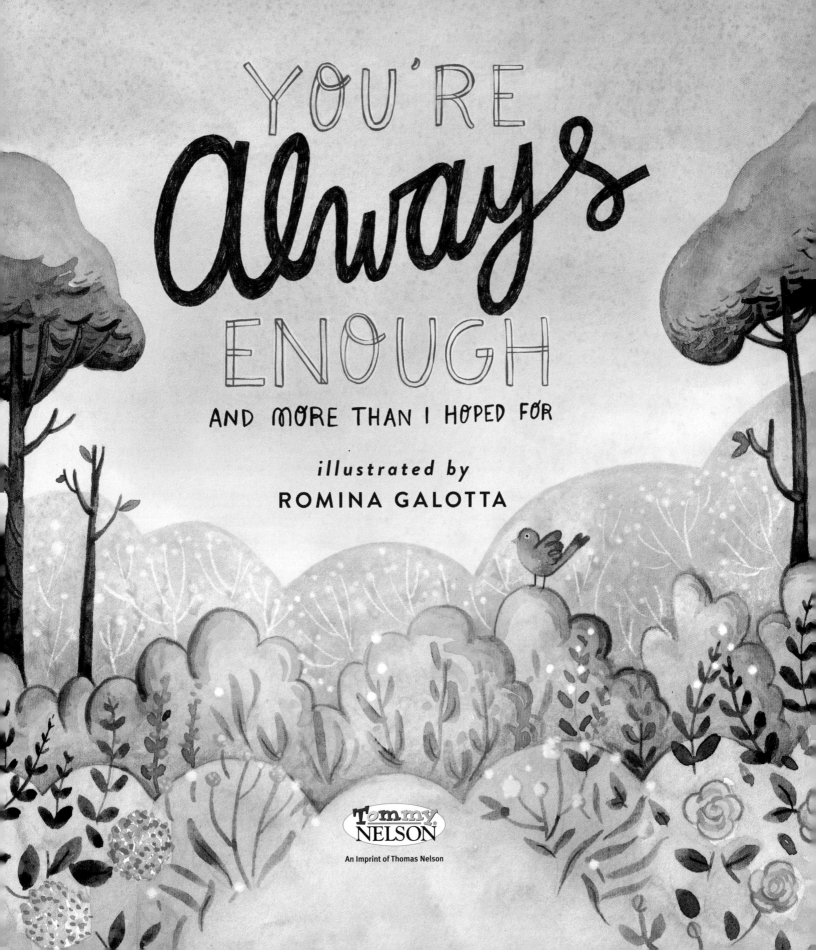

EMILY LEY

YOU'RE Always ENOUGH

AND MORE THAN I HOPED FOR

illustrated by
ROMINA GALOTTA

Tommy
NELSON®

An Imprint of Thomas Nelson

Published in Nashville, Tennessee, by Tommy Nelson. Tommy Nelson is an imprint of Thomas Nelson. Thomas Nelson is a registered trademark of HarperCollins Christian Publishing, Inc.

Published in association with Folio Literary Management LLC, 630 Ninth Avenue, Suite 1101, New York, New York 10036.

Tommy Nelson titles may be purchased in bulk for educational, business, fund-raising, or sales promotional use. For information, please email SpecialMarkets@ThomasNelson.com.

ISBN 978-1-4002-3151-5 (eBook)
ISBN 978-1-4002-3152-2 (HC)

Library of Congress Cataloging-in-Publication Data

Names: Ley, Emily, author. | Galotta, Romina, illustrator.
Title: You're always enough : and more than I hoped for / Emily Ley, Romina Galotta.
Description: Nashville, Tennessee : Thomas Nelson, [2022] | Audience: Ages 4-8
   | Summary: "Emily Ley, bestselling author, founder of Simplified, and mama of
   three, shares her life-giving message of "grace, not perfection" in You're Always
   Enough: And More Than I Hoped For, a parent-child picture book that builds self-
   confidence in children by removing expectations of perfection--because they're
   perfectly loved just the way they are"-- Provided by publisher.
Identifiers: LCCN 2021046102 (print) | LCCN 2021046103 (ebook) | ISBN
   9781400231522 (hc) | ISBN 9781400231515 (ebook)
Subjects: LCSH: Self-esteem in children--Religious aspects--Christianity--Juvenile
   literature. | Parent and child--Religious aspects--
   Christianity--Juvenile literature.
Classification: LCC BV4571.3 .L49 2022 (print) | LCC
   BV4571.3 (ebook) | DDC 248.8/2--dc23
LC record available at https://lccn.loc
   .gov/2021046102
LC ebook record available at https://lccn.loc
   .gov/2021046103

Written by Emily Ley.
Illustrated by Romina Galotta.

Printed in the United States of America

23 24 25 26 PC 6 5 4

Mfr: PC / Hagerstown, MD /
July 2023 / PO #12213698

To Brady, my buddy and my first baby.

You are a delight, sweet boy.

—Mom

To my parents, for their constant support and love.

—R. G.

I never could have asked for more.
God made my dreams come true.
He filled my life with **LOVE** and **JOY**
by giving me sweet you.

No matter what our days bring,
  whether good or bad or rough,
    you'll always be my treasure,
      and you'll always be enough.

Now, some days you'll feel FANCY,

and some days you'll feel BLAND.

At times you'll feel so ANGRY.

And others you'll feel GRAND.

So no matter what you're feeling,
I'm proud of what I see—

you're quirky in my favorite ways,
as **SPECIAL** as can be.

I see your kind and lovely soul.
You're a caring, including friend.

I love how deep you think your thoughts.
YOU'RE ONE AMAZING KID.

When life gets WILD and MESSY,
when choices are hard to make,
when others make you really mad
or you make a big mistake,
just know that no one's perfect,
not me,

not them,

not you . . .

What **MATTERS MOST** is being kind,
sincere, and brave and true.
What matters is your laughter,
your **SMILE**, your **GENTLE HANDS**,
your willingness to be a friend
and **HELP OUT** when you can.

When you have a **TRICKY** problem
or some worries on your mind,
when you're not sure which choice to make
and it leaves you in a bind,
remember who you are inside
and that I'll hold you tight.
The Lord will **GUIDE** your every step,
and He will be your light.

You're **MARVELOUS**
and **MESSY**.

You're sweet
and spicy too.

You're capable
of anything

you put your
heart into.

You're **ENOUGH**
when you are angry.

You're **ENOUGH**
when you're picked last.

You're **ENOUGH**
when you have questions.

You're **ENOUGH**
when you are sad.

ENOUGH !

When someone hurts your feelings
or makes you feel so small,
remember what you're made of—
you're the **YOU-EST** you of all.

Your heart is made of sunshine,

your smile of **RAINBOW** beams.

Your hugs are marshmallows and honey.

Your laugh's as sweet as cream.

And if you start to wonder
if you truly measure up,
remember that you're
full of hope
and goodness,
joy, and
love.

WHAT MORE COULD I HAVE HOPED FOR?

I'm proud to call you mine.

And I'm so glad to have the chance

to love you all my life.

I love to watch you build new things.
You DREAM. You SOAR. You FLY!

You use imagination,

and you try with all your might.

I love to watch you do hard things.
You **STAND UP** when you fall.

But most of all I love the way
you try to conquer all.

There may be rooms you walk into
you're sure you don't fit in.
But you can stand up proud and tall.
Be **HAPPY** in your skin.
And when you worry if you've got
what it takes to be **SO BRAVE**,
when the worries in your head
make you feel a bit afraid . . .

just focus **DEEP INSIDE** your heart
and gather all your strength.
Remember you have what you need
to get through **ANYTHING**.

For God above made no mistakes
when He was making you.
He made you TENDER, TOUGH, and BOLD,
fantastic through and through.
He knew precisely who you'd be—
so WONDERFULLY complex.
He knew the world would need someone
so different from the rest.

ENOUGH does not mean perfect.
ENOUGH's not what you do.
ENOUGH means being who you are—
the way that God made you.
So when you start to wonder
if the parts of you add up,
remember what you know inside . . .

You'll **ALWAYS** be enough.